POEMS
to
POOP
by

POEMS
to
POOP
by

Silly Sonnets, Lewd Limericks,
and Other Bathroom Rhymes
to Pass the Time

brian boone

CASTLE POINT BOOKS
NEW YORK

www.castlepointbooks.com

The Castle Point Books trademark is owned by
Castle Point Publishing, LLC.
Castle Point books are published and distributed by
St. Martin's Publishing Group.

ISBN 978-1-250-32402-3 (trade paperback)
ISBN 978-1-250-32403-0 (ebook)

Design by Tara Long
Images by Shutterstock.com

Our books may be purchased in bulk for promotional,
educational, or business use. Please contact your local bookseller
or the Macmillan Corporate and Premium Sales Department
at 1-800-221-7945, extension 5442, or by email at
MacmillanSpecialMarkets@macmillan.com.

First Edition: March 2024

10 9 8 7 6 5 4 3 2 1

CONTENTS

INTRODUCTION

Here be rhymes
For all the times
You need a good distraction

For when you're seated
And things feel heated
We offer satisfaction

To escape the strife
That fills your life
Pull up to the potty

Then crack the spine
Of this book divine
With poems odd and naughty

Inside you'll find
What we've designed
We hope that it entrances

So pick a page
And just engage
While your bowel health advances

There once was a book of short poems
About some embarrassing low hums.
These incredible rhymes
Helped pass the time
As readers dropped bombs
From their own bums.

LIMERICKS
for the
LAVATORY

THERE ONCE WAS A FARMER NAMED STROOP

There once was a farmer named Stroop
who needed to drop quite a poop.
But the bathroom was taken,
which left Stroop quite shaken,
So Stroop went to poop in the coop.

IN THE REALM OF PORCELAIN AND PIPES

In the realm of porcelain and pipes
Where nature calls to all types,
There sits a throne
Where all may atone,
Causing laughter, relief, and a few stripes.

THERE ONCE WAS A TOILET SO CLEAN

There once was a toilet so clean
Its porcelain had quite a bright sheen.
With a flush that was swift,
It gave users the gift,
Of leaving nothing behind to be seen.

THERE ONCE WAS A WORKER NAMED LOU

There once was a worker named Lou
Who desperately needed to poo.
With his meeting still going,
And to keep folks from knowing,
He just put the Zoom call on mute.

IN THE SHOWER,
A NOTION TOOK HOLD

In the shower, a notion took hold

To pee, in a tale often told.

With a quiet release

And a grin like a beast

He unleashed a river of gold.

IN THE BATHROOM, I TRIED SOMETHING NEW

In the bathroom, I tried something new:
A bidet full of water so true.
With its warm, gentle spray,
My troubles washed away,
And now I'm as fresh as the dew!

IN THE JOHN,
I GOT A SURPRISE:

In the john, I got a surprise:
No paper, despite my loud cries.
I searched high and low,
But it was a no.
With a waddle, I ran for supplies.

THERE ONCE SAT A GUT IN MUCH STRESS

There once sat a gut in much stress;
Constipation brought a sense of unrest.
No relief could be found,
As the days did abound,
But then fiber and prunes brought success!

THERE ONCE WAS A WOMAN, IT'S TRUE

There once was a woman, it's true
Whose bowels refused to pass through.
She sat on her throne,
With a sad moan and groan.
From the effort she turned shades of blue.

IN A RESTROOM
A URINAL STOOD

In a restroom a urinal stood
Where men could whip out their goods.
With aim they'd take pride,
No reason to hide,
They'd shake off as much as they could.

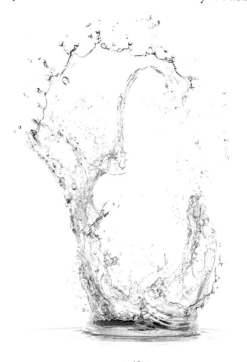

THERE ONCE WAS
A TOILET DIVINE

There once was a toilet divine
Which flushed with a thunderous whine.
It swirled and it spun,
Until the job was done,
And left the room smelling just fine.

THERE ONCE WAS
A MAN FROM VAIL

There once was a man from Vail
Who strolled around town with a pail.
Of the bucket, you're curious,
'Twas both useful and glorious.
"Unlike toilets," he said, "this won't fail."

THERE ONCE WAS A
ROCK 'N' ROLL DRUMMER

There once was a rock 'n' roll drummer
Who found himself needing a plumber.
He had dropped both his sticks,
And then flushed them for kicks.
"Oh man," he exclaimed, "what a bummer!"

THERE ONCE WAS A GIRL IN MY CLASS

There once was a girl in my class
Who during a test had some gas.
She lifted a cheek,
And let out a squeak.
There was no way she ever would pass.

A ballad's like a lovely song,
A lyric's like one, too.
And all the ones to follow here,
Will sing of pee and poo.

BALLADS
for the
BATHROOM,
LYRICS
for the
LOO

THE MUSE OF A MILLION PLUMBERS

In a corner, in such brilliant hues,
Sat a lovely porcelain throne.
A humble seat that one would use,
When one must be alone.

Its flush, a symphony of sound,
A cleansing moment of pure power.
Our worries left to swirl and drown,
A modern plumber's muse and flower.

MY FIXTURE; MY FRIEND

My toilet: unassuming friend,
A fixture in my life,
You serve me well until the end,
You bring support in strife.
So let us make a cheer to thee,
For solace, ease, and peace,
An ally you will always be,
For with you comes release.

HOUSE OF THE CRESCENT MOON

Amidst the woods and open air,
Stands one outhouse, strong and rare.
A rustic dwelling, quaint and true:
A private spot with a lovely view.
Far from a busy city's pace,
It offers peaceful, secluded space.
A humble shelter, weathered and worn,
For nature's call, a place reborn.
A crescent moon carved on the door,
It beckons travelers from distant shores.
A place of wiping, grunts, and sighs,
Under the sun and starry skies.

THE SILENT SAINT

Toilet, toilet, standing tall,
In the bathroom down the hall,
What great comfort you provide,
With a bowl so wet and wide,
What great horrors you have seen,
And still you help to keep us clean.
You take it all without complaint,
You truly are a silent saint.

THE SHAME OF A STAIN

I had to use a neighbor's potty,
I left it stained and oh so spotty.
Despite my skills at being squatty,
It looked like I was being naughty.

It must have been cup number three
Of that strong, dark, and bitter tea.
That stuff moves through me urgently,
And out comes so much more than pee.

FOOL'S CAKE

One time I tried a piece of cake
That a friend claimed to have baked.
It made my stomach turn and shake,
It was too much for me to take.

I wound up in a bathroom stall,
And that's when I realized it all:
This cake I'd eaten wasn't food,
I'd been served a urinal cake, dude!

CREATURE COMFORTS

Potty break,
Happy flush,
Wash my hands,
Good enough.
While I'm standing
at the sink,
My dog pops in
for a toilet drink.

DAD'S OFFICE

A bathroom is a pungent place
That no one dares to bother.
So that's where we can always find
The man that we call "Father."

PANTS OPTIONAL

You don't have to wear your pants
While you're in a bathroom trance.
Just sit right down, take a moment,
Enjoy a break that's extra potent.

PARTY FOUL

While chatting at a friend's big party,
I started to feel kind of farty.
That's when I sought out a route
To a room where I could toot.
But as I walked along while gassing,
Something else came passing, passing.
So here the situation stands:
I'm sadly scrubbing at my pants.

SOMETHING IS AMISS

The floor is sticky, and quite yellow,
Because I had to follow some fellow
Who didn't aim well at the hole
And left his mark outside the bowl.

TELL IT LIKE IT IS

Live, laugh, love, the sign did read,
But that is not the one I need.
If a bathroom ever needed comment,
It'd be: *Enter, sit down, leave your contents.*

LUCKY BREAK

The toilet paper's getting thin
In this public stall I'm in.
I fear I will not have enough,
And I'll leave messy, wet, and rough,
But hark, what does my luck provide,
I'll gladly say I nearly cried.
A worker came by to restock,
I was "this close" to using sock.

Upon my door he gently tapped,
The roll I then quickly unwrapped.
I did my business, clean as a whistle,
And quickly made my own dismissal.
Crisis averted, I thought, relieved,
For the emergency roll I just received.

A WORD OF WARNING

You'll wind up early to a casket
If perchance you blow a gasket.
So take it easy, do not strain,
You're after relief, and never pain.

ABOARD ME VESSEL

Sometimes I pretend I'm a pirate captain,
Sailing on the ocean blue,
But really I'm just on the toilet,
Having a raucous pee and a poo.

I'll yell for the men to fire the cannons,
And fire off one of my own,
Then I hear its mighty splash
From atop my nautical throne.

Ahoy, the mighty double-ply:
I hoist it back behind my thighs.
I flush and raise my pantaloons,
Then, having conquered, leave the room.

LOCK OR BE A LAUGHING STOCK

Today my bathroom has a lock,
So nobody can laugh and gawk.
It goes back to my teenage years,
When I drew the laughter of my peers.
The stalls at school did not have doors,
So all could hear the fanny roars.
So now to avoid gastro anxiety,
I have to ensure total privacy.

A PLEA FOR YOUR PELVIS

Please be careful,
  don't distress.
You should never
  force or press.

Don't push out
  what will not come.
You'll just make
  your butt go numb.

Be kind to your guts,
  and also your pelvis.
Constipation extreme
  is what killed Elvis.

THE END OF THE ROLL

I could not find the toilet paper,
Which got me into quite a caper:
I opened cabinets and drawers
While hunching over on all fours.

I didn't seem to have an option
Before I had a big eruption.
I had to evacuate my bowels,
So, yes, I will replace those towels.

R.I.P. PANTS

I felt the sound of roaring thunder,
That bubbled up from way down under.
And so I didn't even wonder
What had split my pants asunder.

SONG OF A SYNDROME

My bowels being inflammatory,
I found myself a lavatory.
It's really self-explanatory.
A flush, of course, was mandatory.

From ancient Japan:
Haiku—a calming poem
for a pensive poop

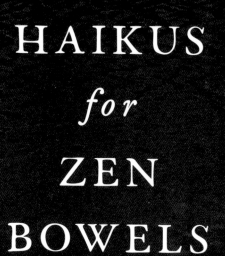

HAIKUS

for

ZEN

BOWELS

I think, then I fart
I return to my thinking
and then a poop blooms

I thought I would pee
alas that was not my fate
oops, no TP here

Installed a bidet
expecting warmer treatment
this throne is still cold

Stomach feels so full
straining, pushing, no release
constipation's hold

Water from below
cleansing with a gentle spurt
bidet, a fresh stream

Air thick with odor
stinky bathroom, oh so foul
hold your breath and flee

Urgent call within
gut in turmoil, twisted knot
diarrhea flows

Sweat drips off my brow
A storm builds in my body
Relax. Bathroom's free

I felt a rumble
Nature was calling loudly
Huzzah! A truck stop

My vegan diet
provides a lot of fiber
ten pounds dropped just now

How lucky we are
to have toilets in our time
Those poor chambermaids

Here I meditate
about life's great mysteries
Oops, it's been two hours

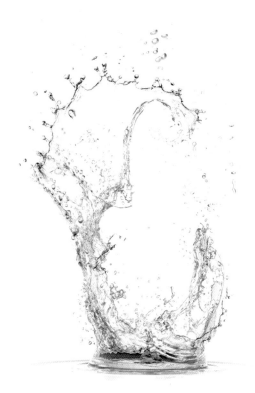

Insta-poetry is an
internet
phenomenon

It's as easy to write one
or read one
as it is
to use
the bathroom

INSTA-
POETRY
for
INSTA-
RELIEF

it's always the quiet ones
who make the most noise
in the bathroom
you don't know what you've got
'til it's gone—
like toilet paper

I hear you knocking
but you can't
come in
trust me

you don't want to

if it stinks in here
I'm not sorry

no one should have to apologize
for what they leave
behind

I carry a flame
for a loved one—
my toilet—
by which I mean

I light a match after

your heart says, you have nothing left
your bowels whisper, press on

shine bright
like the sun
or a diamond
or something
more beautiful—

white porcelain

no regrets—

never

look

back

close the lid

flush

and forget

why do they call it
taking a dump
when I'm not
actually
taking anything
I'm
leaving something

there's nothing sadder
than a broken toilet

we have nowhere
to go

they say soulmates
don't exist
but a toilet
always listens
and takes my crap

I miss
when people had
those fuzzy
toilet seat covers
it was like
        pooping
inside
a Muppet

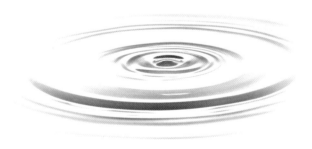

why do they call it
number two
when leaving
your desk
to poop
is the number one way
to get out of work
for a while

I may sit
and do nothing
in the bathroom
but the toilet
is always
running

anything
a man can do
a woman
can do too

unless

it's peeing in the woods
that's so much
easier
for dudes

Hark! What do these sonnets
And the rides at an amusement park bathroom
Have in common?
Both have long lines.

SILLY

SONNETS

for the

POOPER

Sonnet 1:

MY CALM TOILET, YOU INSPIRE ME TO WRITE

My calm toilet, you inspire me to write.
I love the way you beckon me to you,
Invading my mind all day and all night,
So I dream about my next perfect poo.

I'll compare you to a lovely lake,
You are more pristine, glorious and calm.
Bleach makes you bright like the month of June,
On your tank I can lean and rest my arms.

How do I love you? Let me count the ways:
I love your form: tank, seat, and bowl,
I plan around you my meals, nights, days,
To get back to you often, that's the goal.

Now I must take leave with a bursting heart,
Just know I'm coming if you hear me fart!

OH PORCELAIN THRONE, SO OFT NEGLECTED

Oh porcelain throne, so oft neglected,
Yet faithful servant in each abode.
With flushing power quite unexpected,
You take our waste on journeys untold.
From humble homes to the grandest estates,
You bear the burden of our filth and shame.
And though we may flush and walk away,
Your silent service, it remains the same.
Oh, toilet bowl, your gleaming white,
Reflects the truth we cannot ever hide.

A mirror of our innermost dark plight,

In you our dirty secrets do reside.

So here's to thee, dear commode so divine,

For all of the times you've saved my behind.

Sonnet 3:

THIS ROLL OF PAPER, SOFT AND PURE TO TOUCH

This roll of paper, soft and pure to touch,
You stand as sentinel so brave and mighty.
With gentle fibers, strong and white as such,
You wipe away our filth and leave us tidy.
No task too great for thee, paper friend,
You comfort with each careful stroke.
And in our moment of great need attend,
A loyal servant, a flimsy white cloak.

Oh humble roll, so oft taken for granted,
In times of plenty, we waste without thought.
But when supplies fall, we're disenchanted,
And yearn for the comfort thou hast brought.
So here's to thee, dear toilet paper fair,
A simple yet essential perfect square.

Sonnet 4:

IN THIS SONNET,
A TALE I UNFOLD

In this sonnet, a tale I unfold,
Of struggle deep, a plight that's so unkind,
Where nature, once moving, cannot flow,
And in this verse, constipation we find.
Oh, cruel twist of fate, that binds one within,
The wretched clench that holds a gut so tight,
A battle waged, where victory won't begin,
As minutes pass, and daylight turns to night.

The fiber pills, the prunes, they lend their aid,
Yet still, the tides refuse to ebb and flow,
The torment grows, a burden unrepaid,
As straining efforts bring sweet release, no.
But fear not, troubled souls, relief shall come,
Until then, you'll just sit there and be glum.

Sonnet 5:

OF PORCELAIN MADE,
A THRONE SUBLIME

Of porcelain made, a throne sublime,
Where secrets find their sweet repose,
A haven true, where burdens may unwind,
And worries vanish as the water flows.
Within these walls, a sanctuary found,
Where solitude and peace intertwine,
No judgment here, no prying eyes allowed,
Just tranquil moments, rare and fine.

Oh, humble vessel, steadfast and true,
You bear the weight of private scenes,
A witness to the joys and sorrows too,
A tankard where we find our minds at ease.
Toilet, thou art a loyal friend, that's clear,
In moments shared, we find our solace here.

Sonnet 6:

WITHIN THE WALLS THAT HOLD OUR DAILY CARES

Within the walls that hold our daily cares,
A sacred space where solitude resides,
A refuge found when life's burden ensnares,
The bathroom beckons, and relief presides.
Within these hallowed walls, we find respite,
A moment's pause from bustling outside,
A sanctuary where we can rewrite,
The script of life, as worries all subside.

In showers, warm cascades cleanse weary souls,
As water dances gently, pure and free,
In bathtubs deep, tranquility unfolds,
A haven of serenity we see.
Oh, bathroom, thou art more than thy four walls,
Sanctuary! Rejuvenation calls!

Sonnet 7:

AMIDST THE ROOM OF MEN, A HUMBLE STALL

Amidst the room of men, a humble stall,
A haven where relief is nobly sought,
A vessel of release that serves us all,
A place where dignity is never bought.
A porcelain bowl, its purpose so clear,
A conduit for a fluid's descent,
A waiting chalice, men seek you here.
In moments of respite, a moment spent.

Though oft neglected despite its grace,
another statue stands profound,
A witness to our thoughts as we embrace
The silence, as our essence is unbound.
Oh, urinal, unadorned, yet sublime,
In humble walls, a momentary shrine.

Praise be to these odes, a true and earnest
pursuit
To express in emotional poetry, where one
empties their poop chute.

ODES
to the
COMMODE

ODE TO THE JOHN

I think that I shall never see
A thing as lovely as my potty,
A loo whose base is firmly pressed
Against the floor so I may rest
And do my business without fear,
While hoping none outside will hear.

ODE TO SILENT BATHROOM TIME

I am but a bathroom thinker,
This is why I sit and linger,
Staying here for half an hour,
Pondering beside the shower.
I'll stay relaxed with legs so numb,
Until I hear that "drum-drum-drum,"
"What you doing?" they'll call in.
"What happened? Ha, did you fall in?"
"I did not," I'll proudly yell.
What I did, I cannot tell.
I'm just enjoying private time,
Because the silence is sublime.

ODE TO A BROKEN TOILET

Here sits a broken toilet, its functions now
  impaired,
How it took doody as its duty, none shall be
  compared.
Any respect we had, it should be reserved,
For this broken throne, and how it served,
For in its cracks and faded facade,
Lies a tale of resilience, oh so odd.
We find in it a lesson to learn,
About honor, empathy, and concern.
Respect the broken toilet, and you will see,
The power of such decency.
For in respecting the disused, we may find,
A hint of divinity, a world refined.

ODE TO DOUBLE-PLY

Oh, very soft toilet paper divine,
A touch as gentle as the moon does shine,
From cloudlike layers it is made,
To soothe and pamper, a comfort parade.
A tender touch upon my skin,
A chore I cannot wait to begin,
It sweeps away my every care,
Leaving only tranquility to share.
No scraping or roughness do I feel,
Just velvet softness that does appeal.
This double-ply that's fit for kings,
It brings sheer joy to everything.

ODE TO PRUNES

Prunes, oh prunes, let me sing your praise,
For you grace our tables in wondrous ways.
With wrinkled skin and a taste divine,
You bring relief, like a medicine so fine.
When constipation holds back our waste,
And discomfort lingers, you make no haste,
For prunes, yes prunes, doth hold the key,
To set our troubled tummies free.

ODE TO THE DREAM OF A POWERFUL STREAM

In the history of stories, all must agree,
None compares to the tale of the longest pee.
It began when nature called with force,
A bladder so full, like that of a horse.
I was visiting a friend's new home,
When with anticipation, I found their throne.
I stood right there, took a moment to pause,
Eagerly awaiting the relief of this cause.
The stream first trickled, then grew to a flow,
Like a mighty river, I watched it grow.
Time irrelevant, the minutes ticked away,
While friends wondered at my prolonged stay.
The people at Guinness sent forth a decree,
They claimed my pee was a record, you see.
Reporters arrived, so cameras could capture,
My miracle bladder, a biological rapture.

ODE TO THE PERFECT WIPE

Imagine the moment, if you will,
When nature calls, that common thrill.
Into the restroom you swiftly move,
With a mission you're prepared to prove.
With paper in hand, you take your stance,
Preparing for the task, a careful dance.
A dab, a swipe, perhaps a sweep,
To ensure that the aftermath won't creep.
Back and forth, this paper glides,
As you strive for a feeling that surely abides.
You wipe, you toss, you reach for another,
Pampering your backside is worth the bother.
And lo and behold, a moment of glee,
As the paper reveals it's spotlessly free.
No bits, no residue, no smudge or stain,
Your diligence and skill were not in vain.

ODE TO THE FIRST PEE
OF THE DAY

In the early morning, when dawn does break,
I rise from my slumber, my bladder awake.
Groggy and yawning, I stumble out of bed,
The need to pee is strong and urges me ahead.
I stumble down the hall, still half in a dream,
Tripping over objects I hadn't even seen.
I reach the bathroom door sighing with relief,
Knowing that my burden will only be brief.
As I sit upon the throne in this sacred place,
The sound of water brings a smile to my face.
The splash says I've found my peace,
and the day's first task is now complete.

ODE TO MODERN PLUMBING

Indoor plumbing's awfully great
It's something that no one can hate.
Now your toilet's down the hall
Or nestled in a restroom stall.
It wasn't all that long ago—
When it came time to go-go-go,
You had to put on shoes and pants,
And dance your little potty dance
All the way out to "the head"
A tiny, smelly private shed.
The outhouse was your only choice:
For modern toilets, let's rejoice!

ODE TO A SUPPLE ROLL

One-ply was on sale today,
But no, I didn't buy it.
I respect myself and my family too much
to even think of supplying it.
I won't go back, I will not crack,
It's just too thin and bare.
We all deserver a thicker weave,
not one that rips and tears.
I'll always buy the two-ply
Or if they have it, three—
It's self-care in a roll,
And that don't come for free.

Singsong rhymes with farty spins,
'Cause that's the kind of mood we're in.
Poems to move you, bowels and soul.
And parodies for young and old.

A PLOP
of PARODY;
A STREAM
of RHYMES

STOPPING TO PEE ON
A SNOWY EVENING

My Honda Civic must think it queer
To stop without a toilet near
But I had guzzled lots of juice
So I pulled over out of fear.

I ducked behind the biggest tree
And relieved myself—ah, finally!
And from me came the gushing falls
That left behind a growing sea.

The woods are lovely, dark and deep
And I'll just stand here like a creep
With gallons to go before I sleep
Yes, gallons to go before I sleep.

THIS IS JUST
TO APOLOGIZE

I have eaten
the prunes
that were in
the cupboard

and which
you were probably
saving
for when you're backed up

Forgive me
I don't mean to brag
but they left me emptier
than your cupboard

ROAD TRIP PANIC

I worry I will never see
A spot where we can stop to pee.

I've held it in for this whole drive—
How many hours? Four, maybe five?

Soon I know it will leak out:
"I gotta go!" I start to shout.

My dad says, "Son, just hold it in."
My patience, though, is wearing thin.
My pants are getting somewhat wetter,
This will get worse before it's better.

But ho, what is that sight I see?
A rest area! Now I'm filled with glee.

BLOWING OUT THE WIND

How many halls must a man walk down
  before he finds a commode?
And how many farts must escape his bum
  before he can safely unload?

The answer, my friend, will fill you with fear,
  for the toilets are out of order here.

BECAUSE I COULD NOT STOP TO PEE

Because I could not stop to Pee—
my bladder made its plea—
I asked the driver to speed things up—
but it wasn't meant to be.

He slowly drove—he didn't care,
so when I paid the taxi fare,
my bladder leaked all over me,
and ruined my underwear—

TINKLE, TINKLE, IN MY CAR

Tinkle, tinkle, in my car
Rest stop was so very far
Soda bottle just in reach
Glad I grabbed it off the beach
Tinkle, tinkle, in my car
How I needed that glass jar

RING AROUND THE FANNY

Ring around the fanny
For my brother Danny
Pushing, pushing
It just won't budge

Ring around his fanny
Around his major cranny
Trying, trying
He sat for hours

Ring around the fanny
It's really quite uncanny
A circle, a circle
Shaped like the seat

ONE FLUSH, TWO FLUSH

One flush, two flush
Big flush, loud flush
Strong flush, light flush
Can't you see I'm in a rush!
This one will not go away
In the toilet it just stays
See the scary rising mud
Flush again and it will flood
I will need a mighty plunger
This wasn't a thing when I was younger

DUTY CALLS

A soldier walked into the stall,
I followed him and heard it all.
Yes I listened, don't be so snooty:
I had to know if he did his duty.

OCCUPIED

Knock-knock!

Who's there?

I've just taken down my underwear!

Someone's in here, please don't knock.

Can't you see the door is locked?

I'll be done in five minutes, alright?

But possibly ten, even later tonight.

Go away, just let me be,

You'll have to wait your turn to pee!

WHOEVER SMELT IT MIGHT NOT HAVE DEALT IT

Although I was in there for quite a spell,
I can't say sorry for the smell.
I cannot take a shred of blame,
For I am not the one with shame.
Who left the place in such a state,
With odors foul and less than great?
Whoever was there before me, that's who.
Hey, wait a minute—wasn't that...you?

A REAR END RIDDLE

Riddle me this, bathroom user,
Can you name this seaworthy cruiser?
It moves on water; it's not a boat.
It just might sink, but prefers to float.
A mighty whoosh can send it down,
This hearty vessel colored brown.
Can you guess the secret word?
Why yes, my friend: The answer's turd.

RESTROOM REMEDY

When you're down and feeling blue,
Did it ever just occur to you,
That all you need to do is poo?

The source of all that stress and worry,
Can be gone in quite a hurry,
If to a restroom you do scurry.

Now you've answered that aching question:
You've freed up your large intestine,
And found the problem was indigestion.

FANNY FAN

Without a fan, I think you'd see
That bathroom guests would turn and flee,
Because the smells can overwhelm,
'Tis the nature of this realm.

With only the flip of a switch,
The odors retreat without a hitch,
But just in case they don't go away,
'Tis best to buy a fragrant spray.

MARTY FARTY'S PARTY

Marty Farty had a party
In this bathroom here.

Mr. Stroop
Came in to poop,
Then left to get some air.

ROSES ARE RED

Roses are red,

Violets are blue.

The last guy didn't flush,

And now I'm like, "Ewwwww!"

A HAPPY PLACE

In this bathroom, pristine and bright,
I seek solace out of sight,
Near a toilet and a sink,
In a shower where I think.

A haven where I feel so right,
My happy place all day and night.

HOPE IS THE THING WITH PORCELAIN

Hope is the thing with porcelain—
that perches on the tile—
and flushes a tune without words—
and comforts me—a while—

It lifts me to new heights—
and sets my bowels free—
Yet never did it falter—
or complain—about my pee

WATER CLOSET

I followed your directions,
And counted doors I passed,
But I didn't pay attention,
And used the first room, not the last.
So that is why your closet
Is wet and smells so foul.
But, hey, you should be grateful
I didn't move my bowels.

PROBLEM SOLVED

In olden days they used soft leaves, an
  imperfect solution.
A wayward thorn or poison ivy triggered
  evolution.
For we no longer wish to use plants and skins
  and fur,
A gentle wipe that's made to swipe is what
  we all prefer.

DIARY OF A SHARTER

Yesterday I sharted
When I thought I'd simply farted.
My fanny I had guarded,
But the poop, it still departed.
I tried to hold back; I was clearly outsmarted.

THE FALSE ALARM

I can't believe I had the chance,
Now here I sit devoid of pants.
I rushed in here, I had to go,
And now my body just says "no."
A false alarm, I sit and pout,
For I cannot get something out.

A BATHROOM PRAYER

Here I sit,
My bottom under stress,
So please step outside,
I'm about to make a mess.

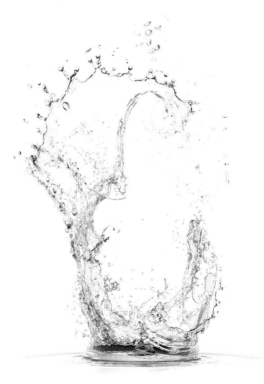